DATE DUE

MAR 2 4 1998	
SEP 2 1 1999	
JUN 0 8 2007	
SEP 7 - 2010	

DEMCO, INC. 38-2931

SECRETS IN
Yellowstone & Grand Teton
National Parks

Published by National Photographic Collections
North Palm Beach, Florida

SECRETS IN YELLOWSTONE AND GRAND TETON NATIONAL PARKS

By Lorraine Salem Tufts

Photographs by Al Buchanan, Roger K. Burnard, Michael H. Francis, Steven Fuller, C.F. Glover, Jeff Henry, Henry H. Holdsworth, Virginia Karrels, Brad Markel, Kathleen Marie Menke, Ken McGraw, Sandy Nykerk, Neil and Trish Ramhorst, Robert H. Smith, Lorraine Salem Tufts

Published by National Photographic Collections

Katie Pelisek and Lorraine Salem Tufts, *Art Directors*

Katie Pelisek, *Designer*

Steven Fuller, Tracey I. Holmes, Sandy Nykerk and Zoe Sanders, *Contributing Writers*

Ellen Koteff, *Consulting Editor*

Tracey I. Holmes and Zoe Sanders, *Assisting Editors*

Barbara P. Brams, *Historical Researcher*

Published in the United States by:
National Photographic Collections
P. O. Box 31355
Palm Beach Gardens, Florida 33410

Printed and Bound by Dai Nippon, San Francisco

Typography by Typo·Graphics, Inc., Orlando
Set in Windsor Light Condensed, Metro Black 2 and Berkeley Oldstyle Medium

Printed in Hong Kong

Softcover
Second Edition
First Edition Copyright © 1988
Second Edition Copyright © 1990
    National Photographic Collections.

Hardcover
First Edition
First Edition Copyright © 1990
    National Photographic Collections.

Library of Congress Cataloging in Publication Data
    Tufts, Lorraine Salem, 1947—
        Secrets In Yellowstone And Grand Teton
        National Parks
    1. Yellowstone And Grand Teton Park—
        Description—Photographic.
    I. Tufts, Lorraine Salem   II. Title
        . .1990   . 90-61150
Secrets in, #1
ISBN 0-9620255-1-8   Softcover Edition
ISBN 0-9620255-2-6   Hardcover Edition

Acknowledgements

The author wishes to express her gratitude to the Grand Teton Natural History Association and the Yellowstone Association for Natural Science, History and Education, Inc.

Special Thanks go to: Sharlene Milligan, Executive Director of the Grand Teton Natural History Association, for her guidance and suggestions; to Gene Ball, Director of the Yellowstone Association, for his suggestions and guidance; to Timothy Manns, North District Naturalist/ Park Historian, for help in seeking identifications and his encouragement; to Bruce Nelson, Professor of Environmental Science at the University of Virginia, for his geological guidance; to Ellen Koteff for her journalistic savvy; Mark Thompson, Editor of Montana Magazine, Inc., for his endless help and information; to Bill Schneider, Falcon Press Publishing Co.; to Steven Fuller for his trust and generous contribution of information; to Michael Francis for his trust; to Paul Pritchard, President of the National Parks and Conservation Association; to Henry H. Holdsworth for his incredible generosity and information; to Bob Smith for his generosity and thoughtfulness; to Barbara Brams for her kindness and patience; to Trish and Neil Ramhorst for their interest, creativity, and enthusiasm; to Tracey I. Holmes and Zoe Sanders for their literary input and outstanding effort on the historical aspect; to Katie Pelisek for her creativity and strength; to Sandy Nykerk for thermal guidance and suggestions; to Roger K. Burnard for literature and encouragement; to Al Buchanan, Virginia Karrels, Brad Markel, Kathleen Menke, and Jeff Henry for their interest and photographs; to Greg Tate, Rosanna Griffin, Louise Mercier, Anne and Buford Potts, Mary Lou and Robert Edgley, Clifford Brokaw, Katie Duffy, Hugh Lane, and Warren Brams; Penelope Edwards; Clyde Hall; Steve Pelisek; Deborah Wardingley; Donald Pharr; Fenstermaker Communications Inc., for constant assistance; and, last but not least, to my mother and father for their instant generosity.

Credits

Contributing writers are Tracey Holmes and Zoe Sanders, page 57. Steven Fuller, photo descriptions, pages 2, 27, and 45. Sandy Nykerk, photo descriptions, pages 12, 40, 43. Ellen Koteff for the Photographer's Profiles, pages 84 and 85; and the Author's Profile, back flap.

The quote on page 80 and the information on pages 80, 81 and 82 is taken from William H. Romme and Don G. Despain in their article, "The Yellowstone Fires", *Scientific American,* November 1989, Volume 261, number 5, pages 37-46 with the author's and publisher's permission.

The Author

Lorraine Salem Tufts has lived in North Palm Beach, Florida for the past eighteen years. Four months of each year is spent traveling and photographing throughout the United States, Canada, the Caribbean, the British Isles, Western Europe, Eastern Europe and Scandinavia.

Her formal education in art began at the age of twelve, continuing to a Fine Arts Degree from Kent State University.

Photography was a hobby her father shared with her as a child. They photographed and worked on darkroom procedures in the black and white lab in their home; however, it wasn't until 1978 that Ms. Tufts started working with a camera again. Fifteen years had been spent as an interior designer and mural painter. Wildlife, scenery, and sporting events are the main subjects of her photographs, with professional status since 1984. She has not actively submitted or promoted her photographs, but has recognition with the Eastman Kodak Company, Palm Beach Daily News, Pine Jog Environmental Center of Florida Atlantic University, the National Park Service, Yellowstone, The John D. MacArthur Beach State Park, Fl., and the University of Virginia.

Secrets In Yellowstone And Grand Teton National Parks is her first formal presentation of her photographs and writing.

Cover Photograph: **DANCING FOXES** *by Steven Fuller, Nikon F3 with Motor Drive, Nikkor 180mm Lens, 1/250 sec. at f5.6, 64 Kodachrome.*

A mated pair taken in late February. Such postures associated with mating season could be dominant/ subordinate behavior. They stood in this position for six to eight seconds before breaking apart. The foxes appeared in the central area of Yellowstone two winters ago.

Title Page Photograph: **OSPREY FLYING INTO THE NEST** *by Brad Markel, Nikon F3 with Motor Drive, Nikkor 400mm 3.5 Lens, 1/500 sec. at f5.6, Tripod, 64 Kodachrome.*

Ospreys build their nests close to water whenever possible. Their diets consist of live fish, which they catch for themselves and their families. This nest was found along Yellowstone Lake in summer.

DEDICATION

TO TRACEY

To youth that has the courage to strive for high ideals, contra mundum.

Lorraine Salem Tufts, Canon F1, Canon 80-200mm Zoom Lens, 1/250 sec. at f5.6, 64 Kodachrome.

MULE DEER FAWN

To the students of Glenn Duncan Elementary School,

Best wishes,

Lorraine Salem Tufts

Oct. 9th 1990

4

Robert H. Smith   Nikon F3   Nikkor 50mm Lens, 1/2 sec. at f16   Gitzo Tripod   25 Kodachrome

ELECTRIC PEAK AT SUNRISE

The secret of this photograph is the perfect moment of morning light from Swan Lake Flat. Patience and a keen eye allowed the photographer to seize the foreground, middle-ground and background with exceptional clarity. The mountain, Electric Peak, dominates the landscape at 10,992 feet above sea level, in Yellowstone National Park.

Neil and Trish Ramhorst   *Nikon FE2 with Motor Drive*   *Nikkor 400mm 3.5 Lens, 1/125 at f3.5*   *Gitzo Tripod*   *64 Kodachrome*

BULL ELK WITH COW IN THE MORNING MIST

Kathleen Marie Menke   *Olympus OM1*   *Zuiko 50mm Lens, 1/2 sec. at f22*   *Bogen Tripod*   *25 Kodachrome*

MOUNT MORAN AT SUNSET
Mount Moran and the Snake River at OxBow Bend during sunset are an awe-inspiring sight.
This mountain stands 12,605 feet above sea level and renders a majestic landscape from Jackson
Lake Lodge, Oxbow Bend and Moran Junction.

Introduction

Yellowstone National Park is located in the northwestern corner of Wyoming with its borders extending north and northwest into Montana and west into Idaho. Directly south lies Grand Teton National Park. Federal law protects and preserves the natural evolution of the geology, fauna, and flora in both parks for the "enjoyment of present and future generations."

The Greater Yellowstone Ecosystem is comprised of national forests, refuges and other federal, state and privately owned lands.

We present a collection of photographs and information about the area. Sixteen photographers exhibit 116 photographs of animals, scenics, wildfire and familiar natural phenomena. They also share secrets on how they created these pictures.

Most members of this photographic group live in the area or are frequent visitors, maintaining the constant data required for capturing certain difficult images. Years of studying the light, animals and environment with patience, curiosity, creativity and respect produced this photographic collection. Most cases of ethical photographic behavior require distance. Large, fast telephoto lenses contribute to wildlife photography by magnifying and thereby offering comfortable and necessary distances for the animals. Sometimes photographers cross-country ski or hike to remote places where they examine signs of wildlife. After checking the lighting, they set-up near a tree or river for the better part of a day, virtually unnoticed by passing animals. It is important to exhibit great patience and stealth, especially when rare photo opportunities present themselves. Feeding animals and setting up a constructed blind are prohibited in the parks, making a knowledge of the area and the species a critical tool gained only after years of work.

Secrets in Yellowstone and Grand Teton National Parks offers an opportunity to own a cameoed collection of sensitive animal behaviors infrequently observed by the average park visitor, newborns, and dramatic portraits, along with breathtaking scenics and hydrothermals.

7

Roger K. Burnard
Nikkor 200-400mm Lens, 1/125 sec. at f16
Velbon Tripod
Nikon F3 with Motor Drive
25 Kodachrome

PAIR OF TRUMPETER SWANS

8

Lorraine Salem Tufts, Canon AE1 Program, Canon 35-105mm Macro Zoom Lens, 1/125 sec. at f5.6, 64 Kodachrome.

FRINGED GENTIAN is the official flower of Yellowstone National Park.

Yellowstone National Park

Lorraine Salem Tufts
Canon 35-105mm Zoom Lens, 1/1000 sec. at f22,   *Polarizer*   *Canon AE1 Program*
                                                       64 Kodachrome

OLD FAITHFUL
DURING SUNRISE IN THE FALL

Old Faithful is the most famous geyser in Yellowstone National Park. Appropriately named by General Henry D. Washburn in 1870, this geyser continues to erupt at fairly regular intervals. At times it reaches the extraordinary height of 180 feet.

10

Lorraine Salem Tufts
Canon 80-200mm Lens, 1/125 sec. at f11

Canon F1 with Motor Drive
64 Kodachrome.

ELK COW HERD RESTING AT OPAL TERRACE, MAMMOTH HOT SPRINGS

Lorraine Salem Tufts
Canon 35-105mm Lens, 1/30 sec. at f16   *Polarizer, Monopod*

Canon AE1 Program
64 Kodachrome

FISHING CONE, YELLOWSTONE LAKE AND THE ABSAROKA MOUNTAINS AS VIEWED FROM THE WEST THUMB GEYSER BASIN

Hot Springs & The Hot Spot

Hot springs are a phenomena often characteristic of a recently active volcanic area. They are a point of release for underground water which has been heated by magma or molten rock. The water temperature is at least 10-15°F (6-9°C) warmer than the air temperature of the area. These springs may represent the last stage of heat loss by molten or partly molten material found beneath the Earth's surface. While slowly cooling, igneous rock gives off high temperature vapors and gases.

Geysers and fumaroles are usually found in volcanic areas. A geyser is a hot water spring which periodically erupts into a fountain. A fumarole is a point of release for fumes and gases. All three, hot springs, geysers and fumaroles, are places where volcanically-heated water escapes. The source of water for geysers and fumaroles is primarily snow and rain. This water, guided by gravity, seeps down cracks, cavities, passages, and tunnels within the hardening level below the thermal area and is heated.

Geysers (from Icelandic "Geysa") discharge ground water heated to the boiling point by extremely hot rocks. Ground water, when held in a chamber and brought to a boiling point below the surface, will violently force out a column of water above it. Consequently, geysers erupt in periodic jets of water and steam. To see the geyser's rapid rush of water, there must be a crack which extends upward and opens at the Earth's surface. After the eruption, the long, narrow opening or fissure fills again with relatively cold ground water, the water heats, and the phenomenon begins again. Many hot springs erupt with regularity—some show periods of violent boiling while others alternately discharge water and gas.

Fountain geysers and cone geysers are the two types of geysers found in Yellowstone. Geyserite, which holds the overflow of water in a pool, forms a basin. A column of water can burst through the pool to create a fountain geyser. Cone geysers have a buildup of geyserite deposits that eventually form the cone around the mouth of the geyser. Higher temperature thermal springs may contain silica which can precipitate and form geyserite cones and terraces.

Fumaroles (from Latin fumus, "smoke") are steam vents. Acidic gases such as hydrogen sulfide and carbon dioxide are typically present. Because the water supply is limited in fumaroles and because temperatures can easily vary, the temperature of a fumarole can fluctuate enormously over time. Solfataras (Italian *Zolfa*, "sulfur") are fumaroles with sulfurous gases. Paint pots, mud pots, and mud volcanoes are also fumaroles. They have a limited water supply and an acidic response. The mud comes from the chemical attack by steam and acidic gases on the surface of the rocks. In addition, the iron present in these rocks gives them a painted look.

Travertine terraces are a form of limestone or calcium carbonate. The hot spring water carries dissolved calcium carbonate held in solution by the high temperature and by the dissolved carbon dioxide. Upon cooling at the surface and losing carbon dioxide, the calcium carbonate precipitates as travertine, which slowly builds terraces such as those found at Mammoth Hot Springs.

Pools are hot springs that do not erupt. They are also formed from the geyserite, but because of their shape, discharge heat by boiling on the surface.

The last of three major eruptions of the Yellowstone hot spot occurred 600,000 years ago. The eruption involving two catastrophic explosions created a large caldera—a relatively oval, basin-shaped volcanic depression—measuring 45 miles long and 27 miles wide. For thousands of years, the lava flow that followed these eruptions formed a magnificent and varied landscape. Most of the geyser basins are in the caldera, as are Lewis Lake, Shoshone Lake, the northern part of Yellowstone Lake, Hayden Valley, and parts of the Yellowstone River.

Subterranean heat, which keeps the park thermally active, may still have other stories to tell. In the larger picture, the Yellowstone hot spot, mentioned above, is thought to be a volcanic plume rising from deep below the Earth's surface. It may be 60 to 120 miles wide and may have been active a minimum of tens of millions of years.

The Earth is not yet middle-aged by the accounts of many geologists. This restless hot spot and all her crowning hot springs have many more dramatic days and nights. For 5 billion more years, the Earth's surface will cool, shift, crack, erupt, split, explode, and sink.

It is estimated that there are as many as 10,000 thermal features in Yellowstone National Park, making this park the largest hydrothermal area on Earth. It is difficult to imagine Yellowstone as a more diverse, more beautiful, or more mysterious place. It is also difficult to imagine it as completely devastated, as has happened before. Whatever the future brings, visiting and seeing Yellowstone is one of the great gifts of our age.

Roger K. Burnard, Nikon F2, Nikkor 80-200mm Lens, 1/125 sec. at f8, Velbon Tripod, 25 Kodachrome

CHOCOLATE POT ON THE GIBBON RIVER

Sandy Nykerk   *Nikon FE2*   *Nikkor 24mm Lens, 1/60 sec. at f8*   *Polarizer*   *Bogen Tripod*   *64 Kodachrome*

SUNSET AT THE LOWER GEYSER BASIN

The sun setting behind the steam plume from Clepsydra Geyser in the Lower Geyser Basin and a dramatic cloud bank contribute to an "other world" effect in this photograph. By scouting locations and anticipating the light, a photographer can greatly enhance the probability of being well positioned.

Man's History In Yellowstone

Because of the determination of a few outstanding men, a geographically isolated area in the Northwestern wilderness of the United States is recognized as one of the nation's most valuable resources for natural phenomenon. This area, called Yellowstone National Park, began receiving public attention as a result of the awe-inspiring photographs, sketches, and descriptive essays from Dr. Ferdinand Hayden's expedition in 1871. Specifically, the photography of William Henry Jackson and the artwork of Thomas Moran inspired congressmen to push through legislation that would preserve Yellowstone for all generations.

Native Americans, the first people acquainted with Yellowstone, had great respect for the spirits that made thunderous noises where the Earth trembles and water boils with smoke. The Crow, Blackfeet, Shoshoni, and Bannock are all credited with knowledge of the area, but it is thought they were infrequent visitors.

One Native American tribe, the *Tukudikas*, did permanently inhabit the area. For their sustenance, they hunted bighorn sheep with horn bows. By all accounts of white trappers and hunters, they were without horses. Osborne Russell, a trapper, observed them as timid, small people living in fear of aggressive outsiders.

By the 1840s, the Northern Shoshoni and Bannock Tribes were forced to visit the country of Yellowstone in an annual search for bison. Their normal herds were disappearing from the Snake River plains.

In 1804, Thomas Jefferson sent explorers Lewis and Clark into the recently acquired territory of the Louisiana Purchase. Although they never entered Yellowstone, a member of their expedition, John C. Colter, did. By 1807 and 1808, his familiarity with the natives and fur trading took his search for new business into the thermal areas, and he is credited as being the first white man to witness geysers and cauldrons. His verbal accounts of Lake Yellowstone were later used on a map by William Clark.

In the 1820s and 1830s, other fur traders entered the region. Daniel T. Potts, overwhelmed by what he saw, wrote the first published description of Yellowstone.

According to historian Aubrey Haines, the acting governor of the Montana Territory, Thomas Francis Meagher, suggested in 1865 that this land should be placed aside for all to see and enjoy.

Finally, in 1869, Nathaniel Langford, a Montana resident and later the park's first superintendent, organized the first Yellowstone expedition. Included were David E. Folsom, Charles E. Cook, and William Peterson. These men were greatly affected by the

Lorraine Salem Tufts, Canon F1 with Motor Drive, Canon 150-600mm 5.6 Lens, 1/250 sec. at f11, Gitzo Tripod, Slik Pro Ball Head, 64 Kodachrome.

BULL MOOSE AT SUNRISE

abundance of natural wonders in the region. Folsom suggested the area be kept free of settlers so everyone could appreciate it as he had.

In 1870, Langford convinced Henry D. Washburn, Surveyor General of Montana, to lead a second expedition into Yellowstone. This expedition brought stories of the Grand Canyon, Lake Yellowstone, and the geyser basins to influential Montana residents. Washburn's party agreed that this land should be preserved. Langford traveled East with his lectures on the uniqueness of the area.

One year later, in 1871, Dr. Ferdinand Hayden of the United States Geological Survey organized a government-backed expedition that included both biologists and land surveyors. More importantly, however, this expedition was unique in that it included among its explorers a photographer William H. Jackson. Also included was the artist Thomas Moran. Their combined artwork brought to the world the natural wonders of Yellowstone and enabled those people who had never seen the area to visualize and therefore appreciate its beauty. The language of pictures helped preserve the area's natural phenomenon by inspiring politicians to advocate laws which would permanently safeguard this environment against future encroachment and exploitation. Finally, in 1872, President Ulysses S. Grant signed a bill passed by the Congress which made government protection of Yellowstone National Park lawful; thus it became the world's first national park.

In 1879, a government headquarters was erected in Mammoth and $10,000 in government funds was provided to protect the land and wildlife from such threats as Indian hunters and white poachers. However, it was not until 1916 that the National Park Service was created. Today, it provides tireless service to the public, the maintenance of the park, research, protection of the natural inhabitants—in fact, the list goes on and on. The National Park Service exercises constant flexibility as geological, ecological, and political circumstances and public information change.

14

Neil and Trish Ramhorst   Nikon FE2   Nikkor 400mm 3.5 Lens, 1/60 sec. at f3.5   64 Kodachrome

CINNAMON COLORED BLACK BEAR
WITH CARRION

Animal carcasses from the winter kill are an important food source for bears in the early spring. This bear was discovered feeding near Mammoth Hot Springs, while alarmed by another black bear watching in a tree. A long, fast telephoto lens was necessary to create this photograph. Although black bears are not as aggressive as grizzly bears, approaching this situation is danger-ous at best and should be avoided.

C.F. Glover   Canon AE1 Program
Canon 70-210mm 4.0 Zoom Lens with Canon 2 x B Extender (420mm), 1/30 sec. at f8
bean bag over car window   64 Kodachrome

GRIZZLY BEAR WALKING IN THE SNOW

This grizzly was photographed from the road at Bridge Bay during a gloomy overcast day in late October. Conditions were poor for a color-saturated picture and yet this shot perfectly projects the mood of the great grizzly's struggle for survival in a world that seems to have little room for him. By thoughtful consideration and desire, humans can find space for this primordial creature to remain wild in the lower 48 states. The protection of Yellowstone and Grand Teton National Parks is hopefully one answer for this native species.

Brad Markel   *Nikon F3 with Motor Drive*   *Nikkor 400mm 3.5 Lens, 1/125 sec. at f5.6*   *Tripod*   *64 Kodachrome*

GRIZZLY BEAR 59 WITH HER CUBS

Getting between a grizzly bear sow and her cubs can be one of the most dangerous situations for humans and animals in the park. Stumbling onto a situation like this is exciting, but best left alone. Give the bear a great deal of room and retreat as slowly and as calmly as possible. Luckily, the river created a natural barrier in this instance.

The secret of this photograph is the length of the lens and the rainstorm. Color is enhanced by water all around.

16

Neil and Trish Ramhorst   *Nikon FE2*   *Nikkor 105mm 2.8 Lens, 1/125 sec. at f11*   *64 Kodachrome*

FEMALE COYOTE

In the ecosystem, coyotes are animals to respect. They seem to adapt to whatever obstacles man or nature presents. Often coyotes are afraid of people and rightfully so, for they have been hunted extensively in the West. In Yellowstone, they are left to their own destiny, unharmed by man. This young female demonstrates the curious side of her nature as she boldly combs the road near Tower Junction on a quiet October morning. The photographers were able to achieve this shot by placing the camera at an unusual angle from their subject.

Ken McGraw   *Nikon F3 with Motor Drive*   *Nikkor 600mm Lens, 1/125 sec. at f5.6*   *Tripod*   *64 Kodachrome*

BOBCAT WITH PREY

Solitary and secretive, the bobcat is rarely seen because it dwells in inaccessible rocky terrain with dense cover. These animals possess keen senses and are known to be proficient hunters. Bobcats prefer to stalk and then leap or pounce on their prey. While not a common sight in the park, this species is part of the Greater Yellowstone Ecosystem.

Neil and Trish Ramhorst   *Nikon FE2 with Motor Drive*   *Nikkor 300mm Lens, 1/250 sec. at f8*   *Gitzo Tripod*   *64 Kodachrome*

FEMALE BADGER WITH THREE YOUNG

Stealth, patience and a long telephoto lens were the tools needed to capture this rare sight. After numerous hikes in Lamar Valley, these photographers found a female badger in the den with her young. After hours of waiting, mother emerged, looked around, and then allowed her three young to come out and play in the sunlight.

Robert H. Smith   *Nikon F3*   *Nikkor 24mm Lens, 16 sec. at f5.6*   *Gitzo Tripod*   *25 Kodachrome*

MOONRISE AT MAMMOTH TERRACES

Taken from Mammoth Hot Springs, this scene shows a small thermal spring with dead trees from the hot water overflow. This, along with the moon and Mount Everts, sets the stage for a beautiful composition. Here the photographer's secret is the constant study of the area and the ever-changing beauty caused by temperature, light, and weather. A compromise was necessary to provide adequate depth of field and still freeze the motion of the moon.

20

Henry H. Holdsworth
Nikkor 400mm Lens, 1/125 sec. at f4   *Gitzo Tripod*

Nikon FE2 with Motor Drive
64 Kodachrome

BISON COW WITH NEWBORN CALF

This bison cow attends her day-old calf during an April snowstorm. Newborn calves are protected by their mothers for the first year of life. After that time, the yearlings must fend for themselves within the herd and in the world at large.

Knowledge is the key to photographing this special moment. Bison give birth in the spring and knowing the activities and movement of the Yellowstone and Grand Teton herds is very helpful.

Lorraine Salem Tufts   Canon F1 with Motor Drive   Canon 150-600mm 5.6 Zoom Lens, 1/250 sec. at f5.6   Gitzo Tripod, Slik Pro Ball Head   64 Kodachrome

YOUNG BULLS SPARRING DURING THE RUT

These bison are young bulls that belong to a herd of twelve or thirteen cows, calves and yearlings. This display is more an exercise in combat than an actual battle, yet it provides action for an exciting photograph with the advantage being the wait and a long lens.

Lorraine Salem Tufts　　　*Canon F1 with Motor Drive*　　　*Canon 35-105mm 3.5 Zoom Lens, 1/125 sec. at f16*　　　*64 Kodachrome*

BULL, COW AND A CALF

A beautiful morning in August provided excellent lighting for this photograph of bison along the Yellowstone River in Hayden Valley. To enhance the image, back lighting was used so the bison would appear dark and silhouetted in front of the river. The passing ducks add further intrigue to this scene.

An artistic approach to picture taking usually adds a romantic aspect to the portrayal of the subject matter.

Lorraine Salem Tufts
Canon 80-200mm 4.0 Zoom Lens, 1/125 sec. at f16

Canon F1
64 Kodachrome

THE LOWER FALLS OF THE YELLOWSTONE RIVER

This awesome 308-foot waterfall can be seen at the Grand Canyon of the Yellowstone. "Piere Jaune" (Yellowstone) came from the early French trappers who fostered this name from the Minnetaree Sioux Indian's term "Mi-tsi-a-da-zi" (Rock Yellow Water).

Henry H. Holdsworth   *Nikon FE2 with Motor Drive*
Nikkor 400mm Lens, 1/250 sec. at f8   *Gitzo Tripod*   *64 Kodachrome*

BULL MOOSE AFTER SHEDDING VELVET

Moose are the largest members of the deer family. Only the males bear antlers, and they use them to compete with other males during the rut.

For three weeks, this photographer followed a herd of bulls. They finally began shedding velvet by rubbing their antlers against the trees. After another long wait this bull came out of the woods in the evening light to feed on willows. There were still a few strands of velvet hanging from his antlers.

Lorraine Salem Tufts   *Canon F1 with Motor Drive*
Canon 150-600mm 5.6 Zoom Lens, 1/500 sec. at f8
Gitzo Tripod with Slik Pro Ball Head   *200 Kodachrome*

COW MOOSE FEEDING ON AQUATIC PLANTS

Moose wade into streams and ponds, submerging their heads to reach the roots and stems of aquatic plants. Animals in the wild often select a diet which achieves an optimal balance between energy intake and the requirements for certain nutrients such as sodium.

Henry H. Holdsworth   *Cambo SCII*   *Nikkor 135mm Lens, 1/30 sec. at f32 1/2*   *Gitzo Tripod*   *Ektachrome 100 Professional*

CANARY SPRING AT MAMMOTH HOT SPRINGS
A sunrise in April illuminates these travertine terraces and displays colors from algae and bacteria.

Steven Fuller   *Nikon F3, with Motor Drive*   *Nikkor 200mm Lens, 1/125 sec. at f4*   *64 Kodachrome*

BULL ELK TÊTE À TÊTE
Although the rut was over, these two bulls were sparring a hard-fought match for no other purpose than the endless jousting for social dominance typical of hooved animals.

28

Jeff Henry   Nikon F3   Nikkor 85mm Lens, 1/250 sec. at f2.8   64 Kodachrome

BULL ELK SHEDDING HIS VELVET

The fuzzy vascular skin on the antlers of the bull elk is called velvet. After five months, a mature bull can have a five-foot rack weighing as much as thirty pounds. By mid-August the velvet dries and is rubbed off by the bull, exposing the horny antler underneath.

C.F. Glover   *Canon F1 with Motor Drive*
Bogen Tripod   *Canon 400mm Lens, 1.4 x Extender, 1/250 sec. at f5.6*   *64 Kodachrome*

COW ELK WITH NEWBORN FEMALE CALF

Elk usually begin calving at the end of May. This cow recently gave birth to this wobbly-legged calf. The calf is trying to follow its mother while steadying itself in the shallow water. Amazingly, calves begin walking soon after birth. This sequence of photographs stirs one's imagination and curiosity as to the communication between the pair.

30

Roger K. Burnard *Nikon F2* *Nikkor 25-50mm 4.0 Zoom Lens, 1/30 sec. at f16* *Velbon SEF3 Tripod* *25 Kodachrome*

MINERVA TERRACE AT MAMMOTH HOT SPRINGS

Travertine, a finely crystalline and massive deposit of calcium carbonate known as limestone, displays the white, tan, and cream colors of the terrace. This, along with the colors from living organisms such as algae and bacteria which grow in the warm waters, create the spectacular natural phenomenon known as Minerva Terrace.

Lorraine Salem Tufts
Canon 150-600mm 5.6 Zoom Lens, 1/250 sec. at f8   *Canon F1 with Motor Drive*
          Gitzo Tripod   *64 Kodachrome*

YOUNG MALE PRONGHORN ANTELOPE

This ungulate is the only animal in the world that sheds its horns as though they were antlers. Both males and females have horns. The male's horns are larger and have more curl. The bony core is permanent, while the outer horny sheath is shed in November or December. The females have horns most of the time, but they are much smaller than the males and are not shed.

Henry H. Holdsworth   *Nikon FE2 with Motor Drive*
Nikkor 300mm Lens, 1/250 sec. at f8   *Gitzo Tripod*   *64 Kodachrome*

BIGHORN SHEEP RAMS

Two rams pose just prior to the start of their mating season. During the rut, rams will vie for dominance in the mating ritual by ramming horns and heads with great force.

Lorraine Salem Tufts   *Canon F1 with Motor Drive*   *Canon 150-600mm Zoom Lens, 1/125 sec. at f5.6*   *Gitzo Tripod with Slik Pro Ball Head*   *64 Kodachrome*

MULE DEER IN VELVET

At the time this buck was photographed, it was traveling in a bachelor herd of three. Its antlers are almost full grown in this late July picture. The buck will rub off its velvet by September and shed its antlers well after the rut in late January or early February.

34

Henry H. Holdsworth, Nikon FM, Nikkor 400mm Lens, 1/250 sec. at f8, Gitzo Tripod, 64 Kodachrome.

BIGHORN SHEEP LAMB

Henry H. Holdsworth, Nikon FE2 with Motor Drive, Nikkor 400mm Lens, 1/60 sec. at f5.6 Gitzo Tripod, 64 Kodachrome.

PRONGHORN ANTELOPE FAWN

Lorraine Salem Tufts, Canon F1 with Motor Drive, Canon 80-200mm Lens, 1/250 sec. at f5.6, 64 Kodachrome.

MULE DEER FAWN

Lorraine Salem Tufts   *Canon F1 with Motor Drive*
Canon 150-600mm 5.6 Zoom Lens, 1/125 sec. at f5.6
Gitzo Tripod, with Slik Pro Ball Head   *64 Kodachrome*

ELK CALF

Henry H. Holdsworth   *Nikon FE2*
Nikkor 400mm Lens, 1/125 sec. at f4   *Gitzo Tripod*   *64 Kodachrome*

BISON CALF

Jeff Henry   Nikon F3   Nikkor 35mm 2.8 Lens, 1/250 sec. at f22   64 Kodachrome

OLD FAITHFUL AT SUNRISE

In this photograph Old Faithful erupts while all is still at the Old Faithful Inn. Every distracting color and shape is covered under a blanket of snow. The snow is illuminated by the golden glow of the early morning sun. The world seems perfect at this moment in this place.

Henry H. Holdsworth
Nikkor 135mm Lens, 1/15 sec. at f45　　　*Gitzo Tripod*　　　*Cambo SCII*
Ektachrome 100 Professional Film

OPALESCENT POOL IN BLACK SAND BASIN

Radiant hues are present from the algae and bacteria and the constant shields of warm water over them. These factors, coupled with the light of the setting sun, create superior color saturation for a photograph or a fortunate observer.

The "bobbi sox" trees also add interest to this picture. The name originates from the white trunks which are formed when mineral-rich runoff from the hot springs invades the area. The trees draw the mineral-rich water into their trunks, and this eventually causes them to die.

Michael H. Francis   *Canon F1 with Motor Dirve*   *Canon 500mm 4.5 Lens, 1/250 sec. at f5.6*   *Bogen Tripod*   *64 Kodachrome*

RIVER OTTERS

River otters are secretive and seldom seen in the rivers of Yellowstone. This mother and her young pup are playing and fishing in the Lamar River. Often river otters will energetically shake the water from their fur, creating a circular spray of water as shown in this photograph.

Henry H. Holdsworth   *Nikon FM*
Nikkor 55mm Lens, 1/15 sec. at f32   *Locking Cable Release*   *Gitzo Tripod*   *25 Kodachrome*

LIGHTNING IN HAYDEN VALLEY

Hayden Valley lies in the caldera, an enormous basin-shaped depression, caused by a volcanic explosion about 600,000 years ago.

Lightning shots look best when foreground is included. It is easier to photograph at night when longer exposures catch the flashes. For day or night, point the lens at the heaviest concentration of lightning and focus on infinity. Set the aperture high and the shutter speed slow using a locking cable release. This photographer let his meter guide his exposure, and he kept shooting until he caught the lightning streaking across the sky.

Al Buchanan   *Olympus OM1*   *50mm Zuiko Lens, 1/125 sec. at f16*   *Tripod*   *64 Kodachrome*

PETRIFIED TREES ON SPECIMEN RIDGE

Specimen Ridge is home to one of Yellowstone's most unique natural wonders: a petrified forest with a number of the trees left standing vertically in groups. These trees were fossilized after being covered by an enormous fall of volcanic ash. With the passing of centuries, the forest re-established itself, the mountains erupted again, and this chain of events continued possibly 5 or 6 times, giving rise to the theory that multiple layers actually exist.

Some of the deciduous tall timber that stood here about 50 million years ago were oak, walnut, magnolia, redwood, sycamore, and hickory.

Henry H. Holdsworth
Nikkor 55mm Lens, 1/15 sec. at f22   *Gitzo Tripod*   *Nikon FM*
     25 Kodachrome

TOWER FALLS
On sunny mornings, a rainbow can often be seen in front of the falls.

Sandy Nykerk   *Nikon FE2*   *Nikkor 24mm Lens, 1/15 sec. at f22*   *Polarizer*   *Bogen Tripod*   *25 Kodachrome*

EMERALD POOL

Located in the Black Sand Basin, Emerald Pool is one of the loveliest thermal features in Yellowstone National Park. The deep green color of the pool is created by the combination of reflected blue skylight in the water and the yellow and orange algae growing on the walls and runoff channels. A hot sunny day and a polarizing filter help the photographer to achieve maximum color saturation.

Henry H. Holdsworth   *Nikon FM*   *Nikkor 28mm Lens, 1/2 sec. at f22*   *Gitzo Tripod*   *64 Kodachrome*

GREAT FOUNTAIN GEYSER AFTER SUNSET

Not all sunsets over the Great Fountain Geyser display this color combination. Continual observation is required to capture the few minutes of available light for creating the color contrast and hues presented in this splendid photograph.

Al Buchanan   *Olympus OM1*
50mm Zuiko Lens, Polarizing Filter, 1/60 sec. at f11   *Tripod*   *50 Fujichrome*

RIVERSIDE GEYSER

Old Faithful may be more famous, but Riverside Geyser is more predictable. Located on the bank of the Firehole River, this geyser erupts with a 75-foot slanted column of water over the river.

Sandy Nykerk   *Nikon FE2*   *Nikkor 24mm Lens, 1/8 sec. at f22*   *Polarizer*   *Bogen Tripod*   *25 Kodachrome*

GRAND PRISMATIC SPRING WITH WHIRLPOOL

Found in the Midway Geyser Basin at over 370 feet in diameter, this hot spring, the largest in Yellowstone, discharges about 560 gallons of water per minute. The brilliant blue of the pool is surrounded by concentric circles of colonies of colorful cyanobacteria creating the effect of a giant circular prism. Direct lighting and a polarizing filter to remove the glare from the water are essential to reproduce the luminous colors.

44

Jeff Henry　　　　　*Nikon F3*　　　　　*Nikkor 35mm Lens, 1/15 sec. at f22*　　　　　*64 Kodachrome*

CASTLE GEYSER ERUPTING IN THE WINTER

This geyser was named by the Langford-Doane Expedition in 1870. The sinter cone is almost twelve feet high with a diameter of twenty feet wide across the top. It erupts at approximately nine hour intervals. In this photograph the bison gather at the Upper Geyser Basin for warmth from the harsh winter temperatures.

Steven Fuller   Nikon F3 with Motor Drive   Nikkor 200mm Lens, 1/125 sec. at f11   64 Kodachrome

ERMINE

In winter, weasels are known as ermine because their fur changes color. Indicative of seasons in transition, the ermine's pelage has changed from summer yellow-brown to stark white. In mid-October, the grasses of the hillside are sun-cured and rimed in frost. Within a week or two, the first of the permanent snows will have covered the meadows, and the ermine will blend perfectly into a snow-capped landscape.

46

Henry H. Holdsworth   *Nikon FM with Motor Drive*
Nikkor 300mm Lens, 1/250 sec. at f 4.5
Gitzo Tripod   *64 Kodachrome*

**GOLDEN MANTLED
GROUND SQUIRREL**

Henry H. Holdsworth   *Nikon FE2 with Motor Drive*
Nikkor 400mm Lens with 1.4 Converter, 1/250 sec. at f5.6
Gitzo Tripod   *64 Kodachrome*

LEAST CHIPMUNK

Henry H. Holdsworth   *Nikon FM with Motor Drive*
Nikkor 400mm Lens with 1.4 Converter
1/125 sec. at f5.6, Gitzo Tripod   *64 Kodachrome*

RED SQUIRREL

Trish Ramhorst   *Nikon FE2 with Motor Drive*
Nikkor 300mm 4.5 Lens, 1/125 sec. at f11
Gitzo Tripod   *64 Kodachrome*

**YELLOWBELLY MARMOT
YAWNING**

Robert H. Smith
Nikkor 24mm Lens, 1 sec. at f8   *Gitzo Tripod*   *Nikon F3*
                                                                 25 Kodachrome

UNNAMED WATERFALL NEAR SYLVAN PASS

To soften the water flowing from the falls and over the boulders, the photographer set his shutter speed at one second. He braced his tripod with rocks in the middle of the stream to secure it. This technique presents a softened picture.

Michael H. Francis
Canon 300mm Lens, 1/125 sec. at f5.6

Canon F1 with Motor Drive

Bogen Tripod

64 Kodachrome

BOREAL OWL

Generally a very docile creature, the small boreal owl is known for its large head. The owl ranges in size from approximately 8½ to 12 inches. A pesky raven revealed the owl to the photographer, making this photograph possible. Yellowstone National Park records indicate this 1986 encounter was the first confirmed sighting of a boreal owl in the park.

Brad Markel   *Nikon F3 with Motor Drive*   *Nikkor 400mm 3.5 Lens, 1/500 sec. at f4.5*   *Tripod*   *200 Ektachrome*

BALD EAGLE

Eagles are the champion visual animals on Earth, having the ability to spot their prey two miles away. Bald eagles are equipped with muscles in their eyes that control lens curvature. This makes them capable of an accurate perception of movement on the ground throughout their flight and dive. They also have an extra eyelid called a nictitating membrane, which is used to clean and protect their eyes.

Bald Eagles can measure up to seven feet, wing-tip to wing-tip, and weigh as much as fourteen pounds. They primarily live on fish, but are known to eat ducks, rodents, and carrion.

50

Brad Markel   Nikon F3   Nikkor 400mm Lens, 1/500 sec. at f8   Tripod   64 Kodachrome

OSPREY LEAPING FROM A DEAD TREE

Osprey catch fish exclusively. They must be careful not to catch fish that are too large for them to bring out of the water. Once their talons clamp on the fish and they start their lift, their legs extend, and this locks their talons onto the prey. It is impossible to release the fish at this point. Their feet have tiny spicules (or spines) on them contributing to a good hold.

Michael H. Francis
Canon 500mm Lens, 1/250 sec. at f5.6
Bogen Tripod
Canon F1 with Motor Drive
64 Kodachrome

GREAT GRAY OWL

Mysterious is the word best used to describe the great gray owl. This raptor measures two feet or more in height with a wing span of approximately five feet. It is the largest owl in North America, and is extremely difficult to spot because it flies silently and blends well with the forest. Being predominantly nocturnal, this daylight photograph is especially rare.

52

Henry H. Holdsworth   *Nikon FE2 with Motor Drive*
Nikkor 400mm Lens, 1/250 sec. at f4
Gitzo Tripod   *64 Kodachrome*

SANDHILL CRANE

A tall wading bird, this species of crane usually stands over 36 inches, and its wing span usually measures from 6 to 7 feet. One characteristic of this bird is its long, harsh, and penetrating call.

C. F. Glover   *Canon F1 with Motor Drive*
Canon 400mm Lens with Canon 1.4 x Extender, 1/250 sec. at f5.6
Zone VI Wooden Tripod   *64 Kodachrome*

GREAT BLUE HERON PAIR ON THE NEST

Spring is mating season for the great blue heron. The males bring the females sticks, which they fashion into a nest. Both parents incubate the eggs until the squabs hatch. Both adults feed their young. Sexes look alike and sex roles in ritual pairing and parental duties are almost identical.

Grand Teton National Park

Ken McGraw   *Nikon F3*   *Nikkor 600mm Lens, 1/500 sec. at f5.6*   *Tripod*   *64 Kodachrome*

BULL MOOSE IN GRAND TETON NATIONAL PARK

On the morning this photograph was taken, two bulls were vying for the attention of a single cow. This male performs a flehmen posture after smelling the female.

Caution must be exercised when photographing in these circumstances because there is a flurry of unpredictable activity coming from all the animals.

The photographer of this picture went unnoticed because he stood near a tree with a long telephoto lens attached to his camera.

Henry H. Holdsworth   *Nikon FM with Motor Drive*   *Nikkor 55mm Lens, 1/60 sec. at f22*   *Gitzo Tripod*   *64 Kodachrome*

MOUNT MORAN FROM OXBOW BEND

The ever-changing play of light, weather and position instills an endless desire to photograph the Grand Teton Range and the various bodies of water near them. This shot was taken on a cold January morning with the temperature at minus 25°F.

The Geological Story

The Grand Teton Range is the youngest of all the Rocky Mountains. Nine million years ago, a north-south crack or fault of approximately 40 miles formed and extended along the foot of the mountains. East of the fault the surface dropped, while on the west side the earth tilted upward. This fault-block process forged the beginning of this magnificent range.

The rock that makes up the mountains is not young. It consists of granite gneisses and schists, formed 2.5 billion years ago, making this some of the oldest, hardest and least-porous rock in North America. About 1.3 billion years ago, dark igneous rock forced through the gneiss and granite, forming vertical dikes. One can easily be seen on the east face of Mount Moran.

A place to obtain a visual understanding of the fault line is from the flat plains to the east of the mountains. From this vantage point, the mountains virtually jut up from the valley floor. The peak of the Grand Teton exceeds 13,000 feet above sea level at 13,770 feet, while at least seven additional Teton peaks surpass heights of 12,000 feet. They are Mount Owen, Middle Teton, Mount Moran, South Teton, Teewinot Mountain, Thor Peak and Cloudveil Dome. In addition, there are many peaks which exceed 10,000 feet in this dramatic mountainscape.

Over time the valley block has dropped four times greater than the mountain mass has risen. The magnitude of this distance, however, is not evident from the Earth's surface because the valley block is covered by sedimentary debris.

The Earth uses many forces from within to sculpt her geological shape: pressure, heat, cracking and shifting. The story then continues with the outer forces called erosion — the wearing away of rock and soil by weathering, water flow, glaciers, and wind. Millions of years of rain fell, with water running down from the high places to the lower places, slowly wearing away and shaping the mountains.

This process continued until a cooling period occurred, (150,000 years ago) allowing snow to fall and accumulate, compact, and remain as ice. Again and again, the snow would fall, melt, and compact until these masses became enormous and very heavy. Gravity

Brad Markel, Nikon F3 with Motor Drive, Nikkor 400mm 3.5 Lens, 1/250 sec. at f5.6, 64 Kodachrome

GRAY JAY

The play of light and tightness of the shot elevates this relatively familiar subject to visual glory. Note the detail of the loose, fluffy plumage which assists the gray jay in silent flight.

pulled them from their high mountain places. They moved great distances and carved the jagged appearance of the Teton Range. Over the thousands and thousands of years, more than one glacier did its work. Ice Age glaciers are responsible for shaping the mountains, carving the valleys and depositing soil, rock, and detritus in the lower valleys.

The last glacial advance, which ended fifteen thousand years ago, left five small, piedmont lakes at the foot of the eastern face of the mountains. Jenny, Bradley, Taggart, Leigh, and Phelps Lakes are held in by morainal dams. A moraine is a mound or ridge of massive rocks or sediment, unstratified in its character, and deposited chiefly by the direct action of glacial ice. The mountains and glacial lakes look very much the same today as they did at the end of the Ice Age.

Alpine glaciers are still supported by the mountains. They are nestled in north or east-facing cirques among the seven highest peaks. These mountain glaciers are not remnants from the Ice Age. They are only about 4,500 years old, originating from what is called the Little Ice Age. Although very small in comparison to the great glaciers of the major Ice Age, they continue to sculpt, carve, and grind the range.

Quartzite rock from glacial material covers the valley floor. This rock, mixed with gravel, sand, and silt, composes the soil which supports sagebrush, grasses, and other arid-adapted plants. Glacial runoff washed much of the clay content from this area, but lodgepole pines grow where the glacial moraines are younger and still rich in clay and nutrients. Water from lakes, rivers, streams, and ponds maintains willow bushes, spruce, and cottonwood trees.

The geological epic is long and detailed, spanning years of study and volumes of written material, yet a cursory look at this story can stimulate the curious and inform the laymen on how this breathtaking scenery was chiseled.

56

Henry H. Holdsworth   *Nikon FM*   *Nikkor 55mm Lens, 1/60 sec. at f22*   *Bogen Tripod, Arca Swiss Mono Ball Head*   *64 Kodachrome*

**GRAND TETON RANGE FROM THE SNAKE RIVER
OVERLOOK ON A WINTER MORNING**

Man's History In Grand Teton

Just as the majestic peaks of the Grand Teton Range inspired the viewers of the past, they continue to instill a sense of awe to the visitors of the present. Because of the harsh winters and geographic isolation, the mountains remained cut off from the white man until the early 1800s. Even the nomadic Indian tribes, including the Bannock, Crow, Nez Pierce, Gros Ventre, and Shoshoni, who were natives of the area, could not tolerate the rigors of the Grand Teton winters.

In 1807 a fur trader named John Colter left the Lewis and Clark expedition to continue his search for fur-trading Indians. This search lead him to the Gros Ventre mountains from where he could see the Grand Teton Range, making him the first known white man to gaze upon these awesome peaks. Unfortunately, because Colter was a trapper and fur trader, he did not document any of his discoveries. The valley of the Grand Teton Range received its name, "Jackson's Hole," from Bill Sublette and "Davey" Jackson who, like Colter, preferred to trap in this area. By the 1840s, however, the various trappers and explorers began to leave the region, and not until forty years later did people begin to settle the region permanently. A U.S. government survey expedition involving some of the most prominent explorers began in 1872. Artist Thomas Moran captured in his sketches the beauty and reality of the mountains. U.S. geologist F.J. Bradley and his assistant, W.R. Taggart, gathered scientific data, and the legendary guide, Richard Leigh, better known as "Beaver Dick," successfully led the group through the area.

Many of the permanent settlers of the late 1880s included groups of varying interests. The cattlemen wanted to protect the grazing land from sheep; other concerned settlers wanted to protect the elk and other wildlife from profit-seeking hunters as well as sportsmen. There were also those that had an ability to recognize potentially long-term problems. Some men began to worry that the influx of

people would alter the ecosystem to such an extent that the environment would suffer irreparable damages. Already changes had occurred which had caused a breakdown in the food chain of the wandering elk herds. Unfortunately, the need to preserve this area's wildlife did not become a public issue until 1918, and not until 1929 did Congress vote to create a Grand Teton National Park.

One of the most successful men to carry out this desire to preserve the Teton wilderness was John D. Rockefeller. The deep concerns of Horace Albright, Superintendent of Yellowstone National Park, and a handful of concerned residents of Jackson Hole stirred a dream in Rockefeller's soul which prompted him to safeguard the land from commercialization and various other forms of exploitation. Through a land company, Rockefeller slowly acquired vast portions of the Jackson Valley. Although the years were tumultuous and

difficult, he and his family continued to achieve this goal.

President Franklin D. Roosevelt established by proclamation the Jackson Hole National Monument to contain those lands purchased by Rockefeller. In 1950 the monument lands were added to the Grand Teton National Park.

Because of the overwhelming beauty and appeal of the Grand Teton Range, the exploration and desire to preserve the region became a personal goal for many. These individuals hoped that all people would recognize our dependence on as well as the intrinsic value of nature. They understood man's relatively fragile and young existence within nature and therefore insisted that our nation not try to conquer the environment, but instead try to live in harmony with it. They understood that if man preserved the environment, he would also preserve his place in it.

57

Henry H. Holdsworth   Nikon FM   Nikkor 28mm Lens, 1/30 sec. at f22   Gitzo Tripod   64 Kodachrome

**THE GRAND TETON RANGE
FROM AN OLD CABIN**

58

Neil and Trish Ramhorst   *Nikon FE2 with Motor Drive*   *400mm 3.5 Lens, 1/125 sec. at f3.5*   *Gitzo Tripod*   *64 Kodachrome*

KIT RED FOXES JUST OUTSIDE THEIR DEN

Photographing fox is very difficult because they are so secretive and there are not many around.

Although these foxes are called "red," they come in many colors such as reddish-brown, reddish-gold, brownish-yellow, silver-tipped mixed with pure black, and black. These different colorations all share the usual characteristic of the white tail tip.

This photograph was taken in the Greater Yellowstone Ecosystem with the vixen close by. The photographers used stillness and a natural blind as their allies.

Lorraine Salem Tufts *Canon T-90* *Canon 85-300mm 4.5 Lens, 1/500 sec. at f4.5* *Monopod* *200 Kodachrome*

COYOTE POUNCING ON A MEADOW VOLE

Coyotes are graceful hunters, capturing small rodents and other prey with quick leaps or pounces. They are invaluable for controlling rodent populations throughout Grand Teton and Yellowstone National Parks. Highly respected by many naturalists, the coyote has earned admiration for its unyielding resilience to survive.

60

Neil Ramhorst *Nikon FE2* *Nikkor 200mm Lens, 1/125 sec. at f8 2/3* *64 Kodachrome*

Trish Ramhorst *Nikon FE2*
Nikkor 300mm Lens, 1/125 sec. at f8 2/3 *Gitzo Tripod* *64 Kodachrome*

LONG-TAILED WEASELS

Long-tailed weasels are the largest of all weasels. Males are larger than females, weighing as much as nine ounces. Their summer pelage is brown on top and yellowish underneath. In winter, they turn white to blend with the snow.

The second photograph shows a standing weasel looking out over the glacier lilies.

Kathleen Marie Menke   *Olympus OM1*   *Zuiko 50mm Lens, 1/60 sec. at f22, Polarizing Filter*   *Bogen Tripod*   *25 Kodachrome*

JENNY LAKE AND MOUNT TEEWINOT

Jenny Lake is the result of glacial ice, flowing from the canyons of the Tetons, which created a basin-formed lake. Similarly, Leigh, Bradley, Taggart, and Phelps Lakes, often called the little jewels of the park, are glacial lakes. In the background Mount Teewinot rises overhead at 12,325 feet.

Lorraine Salem Tufts　　　*Canon F1 with Motor Drive*　　　*Canon 400mm Lens, 1/60 sec. at f5.6*　　　*Stump Mount*　　　*64 Kodachrome*

YOUNG MOOSE EATING WILLOWS

Moose are the least sociable of all members of the deer family in the Greater Yellowstone Ecosystem. This youngster was meandering through the willows, eating alone on an evening late in May.

C.F. Glover
Canon 400mm 4.5 Lens, 1/500 sec. at f5.6   *Bogen Tripod*   *Canon F1 with Motor Drive*
64 Kodachrome

COW MOOSE WITH CALF

This delicate moment took tremendous patience to capture on film. The photographer set his tripod near some willow brushes and waited for hours. Finally, this three- or four-day-old female calf emerged with her mother, who attempted to familiarize her with the river water.

A natural blind is acceptable for photographing wildlife in the parks, but a constructed blind is prohibited.

Virginia Karrels   Olympus OM1   Zuiko 50mm Lens, 1/60 sec. at f16   Tripod   64 Kodachrome

HIDDEN FALLS

The hike to Hidden Falls is short and popular, but the 250 foot drop of the falls is well worth the effort. It is an ascending hike with glacier-polished rocks, green forests, marmots, other wildlife and the sounds of rushing water.

Lorraine Salem Tufts   *Canon F1 with Motor Drive*   *Canon 150-600mm 5.6 zoom Lens, 1/125 sec. at f5.6*   *Gitzo Tripod*   *64 Kodachrome*

BISON YAWNING

This photograph was taken during the height of the rut, yet this young bison was undisturbed by all the activities.

Bison males usually do not mate until their fifth year when they are strong enough to dominate other males. Females are receptive to breeding by their second year.

C. F. Glover   Canon F1   Canon 70-210mm 4.0 Zoom Lens, 1/125 sec. at f11   Zone VI Wood Tripod, Cable Release   Fujichrome 100

MOUNT MORAN AT MOONSET AND SUNRISE

The only way to obtain a photograph like this one is to rise very early, dress very warmly, and keep the camera warm to avoid battery problems. Moonset over the Grand Teton Range during a winter sunrise is spectacular subject matter to capture on film.

Neil and Trish Ramhorst *Nikon F2AS*
Nikkor 500mm Lens, 1/500 sec. at f5.6 1/2 *Gitzo Tripod* *64 Kodachrome*

IMMATURE BALD EAGLE

After five years of seasonal molting, the bald eagle gradually evolves a snow white head, neck, and tail. It also develops a yellow bill from the brownish-yellow one of its youth.

Brad Markel
Nikkor 400mm, 1/500 sec. at f5.6   *Tripod*   *Nikon F3 with Motor Drive*
                                                             64 Ektachrome

OSPREY IN FLIGHT

An excellent field identification for an osprey is the noticeable bend in its wing at the elbow, as shown in this photograph. Osprey are smaller than bald eagles, and not friendly neighbors. When bald eagles build their nests in proximity to osprey nests, stealing fish from ospreys may occur.

Neil and Trish Ramhorst   *Nikon FE2*
Nikkor 600mm Lens, 1.4 Teleconverter (840mm), 1/250 at f8 2/3   Gitzo Tripod   64 Kodachrome

OSPREY

The female osprey does most of the incubation of the eggs while the male fishes for his mate. A mated pair have an admirable working relationship that usually lasts until one dies.

Ken McGraw   Nikon F3   Nikkor 43-86mm Lens, 1/125 sec. at f5.6   64 Kodachrome

IMMATURE RED-TAILED HAWK ON THE NEST

Buteos are hawks of the plains, open woodlands, fields, and mountains. Their diet consists mainly of rodents; however, red-tailed hawks will kill snakes, skunks, lizards, and other ground-dwelling prey. The nest of this five-week-old immature and its parents showed evidence of chipmunk, rabbit, and even marmot remains surrounding it.

Henry H. Holdsworth   *Cambo SCII*   *Nikkor 135mm Lens, 1/15 sec. at f45*   *Gitzo Tripod*   *Ektachrome 100 Professional*

THE CATHEDRAL GROUP
FROM THE OLD PATRIARCH TREE

Ken McGraw   Nikon F3   Nikkor 300mm Lens, 1/500 sec. at f5.6   Gitzo Tripod   64 Kodachrome

CANADA GEESE WITH GOSLINGS

Canada geese are usually migratory, yet many spend the winter in the Grand Teton and Yellowstone National Parks. These geese mate for life and courtship begins in April. Both adult geese share the responsibilities of caring for the young. The gander drives off intruders while the goose incubates the eggs in the nest. Geese eat vegetation from streams and lakes, in addition to grass and other grazing foods. During the nesting season, the adults go into a molt and are unable to fly for approximately three weeks. Immediately after hatching, the goslings are able to swim and feed themselves. The adults, however, will not leave their sides until the goslings can fly.

Henry H. Holdsworth   *Nikon FE2*   *Nikkor 400mm Lens with 1/4 x Teleconverter, 1/25 sec. at f8*   *Gitzo Tripod*   *64 Kodachrome*

WHITE PELICANS AT SUNSET

The contrast of light and dark does more than register subject matter. It creates a mood.

The photographer caught these pelicans preening themselves during sunset on a sandbar at Oxbow Bend. White pelicans fish while they swim on the surface of a lake or stream. They virtually scoop fish into their large pouch. Beautiful in flight, these are extremely large birds with a wing span often as wide as nine feet.

Great care must be exercised to insure their safety and tranquility during nesting and caring for their young.

Henry H. Holdsworth
Nikkor 400mm Lens, 1/500 sec. at f8
Gitzo Tripod
Nikon FE2 with Motor Drive
64 Kodachrome

TRUMPETER SWAN

Grand Teton and Yellowstone support the largest of waterfowl. Grace and elegance best describe the movement of the trumpeter swan.

Once nearly extinct, these swans are struggling to maintain a stable population. They need special conditions for breeding and a lot of privacy. Great care must be taken when photographing trumpeter swans. A small infraction could become a major problem for this species.

Brad Markel   *Nikon F3 with Motor Drive*   *400mm 3.5 Lens, 1/125 sec. at f8*   *Tripod*   *64 Kodachrome*

GREAT BLUE HERON

The great blue heron wades in shallow water, waiting patiently for unsuspecting fish, frogs, snakes and other aquatic life small enough for it to swallow. The heron featured in this picture has a fish in its throat from its most recent catch.

Once great blue herons have survived their first year, they can have a long life, usually ten years, and sometimes spanning up to fifteen or twenty years.

Al Buchanan   *Olympus OM1*   *Zuiko 40mm Lens, 1/250 sec. at f16*   *64 Kodachrome*

LAKE SOLITUDE

Lake Solitude cannot be photographed without a 7.2-mile hike from the west shore boat dock on Jenny Lake. The Hidden Falls Foot Trail starts near there and leads to Cascade Canyon, to the Forks of Cascade Creek, and finally to Lake Solitude. Along the way, a view of Hidden Falls, Inspiration Point, glacial moraines, Teewinot Mountain, Grand Teton, Mount Owen, and Cascade Canyon's glacial sculpturing can all be enjoyed and studied. Also worth mentioning are the wild flowers, pikas, marmots and white crowned sparrows.

Overnight camping is not permitted at Lake Solitude, so it is best to discuss your course of action with a Park Ranger before attempting this adventure.

76

C. F. Glover   *Canon F1 with Motor Drive*

Canon 70-210mm Macro Zoom Lens on a 25mm Tube, 1/500 sec. at f11

Homemade Electronic Cable Release, Zone VI Wood Tripod   *200 Kodachrome*

FEMALE HUMMINGBIRD

Calliope, broad-tailed, rufous, black-chinned and rivoli's hummingbirds have all been seen in Grand Teton National Park. Yellowstone lists rare sightings of calliope, broad-tailed and rufous hummingbirds.

Ken McGraw
Nikkor 55mm Macro Lens, 1/60 sec. at f8   *Portable Flash*   *Nikon F3*
64 Kodachrome

ROBIN'S EGGS HATCHING

This nest was just four feet off the ground and built into the pocket of a cottonwood tree. The mother robin was incubating four blue eggs the first time the nest was discovered. After a few days, three of the babies were emerging from the eggs.

Different species of birds have varied levels of tolerance to human intrusion around the nesting site. Knowledge about the individual species can avoid pressure on the nesting birds.

Kathleen Marie Menke   *Olympus OM1*   *Zuiko 50mm Lens, 1/2 sec. at f22*

**A SILHOUETTE OF THE GRAND TETON
MOUNTAINS BEFORE NIGHTFALL IN AUTUMN**

Fire & Regrowth

IMAGES FROM THE 1988 FIRES IN THE GREATER YELLOWSTONE AREA

Photographs by LORRAINE SALEM TUFTS

Smoke billows over Yellowstone Lake near Grant Village.

Fire destroys signs and trees along the road at West Thumb.

Most animals instinctively move away from the threat of fire.

A conflagration can create its own weather.

Fire burns through the night.

25,000 fire fighters and 117 aircraft worked on the fires.

The Greater Yellowstone Area consists of two National Parks and parts of six National Forests.
This area drew the largest fire suppression effort ever undertaken in the United States. The fires
of 1988 created more national attention in the area than any other event in its history.

SUNSET DURING A FIRE SEASON

SMOKE OVER YELLOWSTONE LAKE

In response to the 1988 fires, two independent teams of land managers and scientists were appointed by the secretaries of the interior and agriculture and by the National Park Service to assess aspects of fire management and control in the Yellowstone area. The two groups, the Fire Management Policy Review Team and the Greater Yellowstone Area Post-Fire Ecological Assessment Panel both concluded that "some kind of natural-fire program, in which lightning-caused fires are allowed to burn under certain conditions, is appropriate and necessary for maintaining the wilderness value of parks and other refuges."

The Christensen report, submitted by the Greater Yellowstone Area Panel, further emphasized the fact that although large fires have burned in the past, this fact alone does not legitimize their existence today. This is because our wilderness areas are much smaller and more confined than they used to be.

Henry H. Holdsworth

Young forests, which replace those burned only a few years previously, usually experience a great diversity of species. In fact, certain species seem to thrive after the event of a fire. Purple fireweed and other herbaceous species are often the first to grow on the floor of a recently burned forest. Moisture is needed to assist in the rapid growth of species. Those areas which are less moist and fertile may follow those with more moisture by several years.

As a consequence, the 1988 fires left areas of ground covered by a layer of ashes. These ashes provide fertilizer for plants which will eventually resprout in the ensuing years, as shown in these photographs.

The Greater Yellowstone Ecosystem

"The Earth does not belong to man; man belongs to the Earth... Man did not weave the web of life, he is merely a strand in it. Whatever he does to the web, he does to himself." These words are credited to Chief Seatlh of the Swuamish Tribe. The Native American had a reverence for preserving the Earth, and he and his people lived it. White men seem reluctant to accept this thought, even with more and more documented evidence of endangered species and animal extinction in our country. Aldo Leopold addressed the problem in 1949 when he wrote, "We abuse land because we regard it as a commodity belonging to us. When we see land as a community to which we belong, we may begin to use it with love and respect."

Our young nation found it difficult to imagine that nature would be finite. With millions and millions of acres to consume, there was no thought of the greater picture. The near extinction of the bison exemplifies this misunderstanding.

The thoughts and philosophies of a man like John Muir were unusual, and yet in the mid 1800s, President Abraham Lincoln had the foresight to sign a bill appointing jurisdiction over Yosemite Valley to the state of California. Theodore Roosevelt also pointed out "that a nation is obligated to manage its resources for the greater good of the greatest number over the long run."

Each of these men and others like them carried the spirit of the Earth in their souls, each passing the torch to the next generation. And yet, it seems something was lost in the transition, because our natural world is dwindling, and it is mostly man-induced. Destroying or distorting one part of the natural world can trigger a chain reaction which takes years to discover, trace back, and solve. Sometimes, the remedy arrives too late.

Today, there is an awareness that Yellowstone and Grand Teton National Parks need more space to protect the wildlife. The Greater Yellowstone Ecosystem is becoming a common term among conservationists, scientists, park officials, and, hopefully, the general public. The term *ecosystem* means the result of interactions between the Earth's biological, chemical, and physical systems. The Greater Yellowstone Ecosystem comprises the two parks, surrounding national forests, various wildlife refuges, and other federal, state and private lands, yet the protection of wildlife and the land is incomplete. The grizzly bear, trumpeter swan, bison, white pelican, coyote, bald eagle, bobcat, elk, black bear, and other species need the safety of the whole ecosystem to prosper. Careful studies, unhampered ancient migration routes, various nesting areas, undisturbed habitat and certain plant and animal availability are imperative for the true stewardship of the area.

Yellowstone, once an area just for witnessing thermal activities, has slowly become one of the last habitats for certain species. This message from nature cannot be ignored. It must be studied, contemplated, and argued to a workable solution.

Our nation's land philosophy once advocated use and dispose, but is gradually turning toward an attitude of learning to conserve, preserve, and replace. Scientific principles should manage the ecosystem and preserve scenic wonders with the protection of law. This can help our commitment to retain this natural world for the enjoyment of future generations of human and wildlife inhabitants.

C. F. Glover   Canon AE1 Program   Canon 70-210mm 4.0 Macro Zoom Lens, 1/60 sec. at f4   64 Kodachrome.

COMMON INDIAN PAINTBRUSH
The official state flower of Wyoming.

Photographers' Profile

84 **AL BUCHANAN'S** assignments have taken him to the Inca fortress of Machu Picchu in Peru, the festival of the Black Christ in Guatemala, and the two-thousand-year-old rice terrace of the Philippines' mountain tribes. But there's no place like home for this young photographer. "The natural spectacles of Greater Yellowstone Ecosystem will remain my first love," says Mr. Buchanan.

ROGER BURNARD started taking pictures in 1957. His professional experience in teaching, biology, photography, zoology, and computers is extensive. Burnard has traveled the world, always with a camera.

His photos have been published in more than 130 textbooks and popular articles. His first visit to Yellowstone was in 1952, but 26 years would pass before he would see the park again. "I understood a bit more about some of the complex interactions occurring in the park

on my second visit," Mr. Burnard says. He visited the park again in the summer of 1987.

MICHAEL FRANCIS has more than ten years of professional experience in wildlife photography.

His photos have appeared in more than seventy-five magazines including *Field & Stream*, *Outdoor Life*, *Montana Outdoors*, *National Parks Magazine*, *North American Hunter*, and *Mainstream*.

Mr. Francis is also the featured photographer in the video, "How To Photograph Wildlife By Eastman Outdoor World." His photos also appear in numerous books.

In the last 15 years, Mr. Francis has photographed extensively in Yellowstone National Park.

STEVEN FULLER has lived in the central part of Yellowstone National Park since 1973 with

his wife, Angela, and their two daughters. Steven received his education at Antioch College, U.S.A., Leeds University, England, the University of Besancon, France, and Makere University, Uganda. He has traveled and lived in various places in North America, Europe, Africa, and Asia.

Mr. Fuller's photographs and writings have appeared in many National Geographic publications including a twenty-eight page story he wrote and photographed for *National Geographic Magazine*.

His photographs and writings have also appeared in various *Audubon* publications and in many national magazines including *Geo*, *Natural History*, *Sports Afield*, *Science Digest*, *National Wildlife*, *Sierra*, and in books published by *Sunset*, *Time-Life*, *National Wildlife Society*, *Reader's Digest*, and in various textbooks and house organs.

He has achieved honors in professional international competitions, most notably in London, England, where he won first place and two other awards in the International Wildlife Photographer of the Year Competition.

C. F. GLOVER is strictly a self-taught photographer. His former hunting and outdoor experience is a great help to him when he works with wildlife. He no longer hunts with anything but the camera.

C. F. Glover resides in Jackson's Hole, Wyoming, where he is active in wildlife conservation efforts. The Happy Peasant Gallery, where he exhibits some of his work, is owned by Mr. Glover and his wife, Cathleen.

C. F. Glover, Canon AE1 Program, Canon 400mm 4.5 Lens, 1/125 sec. at f4.5, Car Brace, 64 Kodachrome.

COYOTE
Female coyotes choose their mate. Even if two males are fighting over a female and one wins, it does not mean she is his prize. Once a male is selected, they usually mate for life. The male provides for the female when she is gravid. The pair is dedicated to one another even though they live in separate dens.

JEFF HENRY has made Yellowstone his home for the past 11 years, photographing and studying nature. He is a seasonal Park Service Ranger and is also a member of The Bear Study Team for the Interagency Grizzly Bear Study.

After graduating from the University of Maryland with a degree in Frontier History and Geography, Jeff headed west and took his cameras with him.

HENRY H. HOLDSWORTH has been a freelance photographer since graduating from Hartwick College, Oneonata, New York in 1982.

He has traveled and photographed extensively throughout the United States. Along with wildlife photography, he also specializes in the art of large format black and white landscapes.

Mr. Holdsworth has exhibited his work in may different galleries and has been published in several magazines and calendars including *Audubon, Wyoming Wildlife, Florida Wildlife,* and *Teton Magazine.*

"Northwestern Wyoming is an incredibly beautiful and unique area. It is as close as you can come to a truly wild place in the continental United States," says Henry.

He now makes his home in Jackson, Wyoming.

VIRGINIA KARRELS became involved with photography 15 years ago on her first visit to the Teton Range. Equipped with only an inexpensive camera, Ms. Karrels became enchanted with the area's beauty. The next year, she purchased her first 35mm camera. She is self-taught in the art of photography and didn't start until she was over 40. Her secret, "Trial and error and a lot of reading and listening."

BRAD MARKEL is a photojournalist working out of Washington, D.C. He has worked professionally for the past nine years with works appearing in every national magazine. Recently, his photographs have been published in *Vanity Fair, Time, Newsweek, Life, People, Fortune,* and *Business Week.*

Wildlife photography is Mr. Markel's

first love, and this is his first professional submission in this field.

K. D. MC GRAW was introduced to the woods at an early age, and moving to Western Colorado in 1972 heightened his awareness of nature and led to his interest in photography.

In 1976, Mr. McGraw pursued his love of photography at Colorado Mountain College, receiving his degree in 1978.

He now earns his living as a nature photographer. "Success in this business is a difficult thing to measure, but I would not trade what I do for a living for another line of work."

KATHLEEN MARIE MENKE has lived in Colorado for 24 years. Following her graduation from college with a B.A. in teaching, Ms. Menke took up writing and photography.

Her photographic training includes numerous courses in technique. Many of her photos are exhibited in galleries.

Ms. Menke uses a simplistic approach to her art. "I look for the essence of the scene and avoid including unnecessary clutter."

She visits the Jackson Hole Yellowstone area at least three times a year, preferring spring, fall, and winter for the best photo opportunities.

SANDY NYKERK was raised in the Rio Grande Valley of Texas on the Mexican border. Because of the climate, almost all activities were based on being outside and led to an early discovery of the natural world.

Ms. Nykerk majored in chemistry while attending college and was later encouraged into photography. She enrolled in photography classes and found her interest in the interpretation of the natural world with the camera.

She first came to Yellowstone in 1980. Each subsequent year, longer stays kindled a fascination with the geology and natural history which brought her to the Yellowstone Institute.

She started teaching workshops in 1983 and added the Yellowstone tour in 1984. She emphasizes man as a part of the natural world, not apart from it, actively working on the Board of Directors of the Greater Yellowstone Coalition. She exhibits her work in Chicago salons and has been awarded for her photography.

Henry H. Holdsworth, Nikon FE2 with Motor Drive, Nikkor 400mm Lens with 1.4 x Converter, 1/250 sec. at f5.6, Gitzo Tripod, 64 Kodachrome.

P I K A

NEIL RAMHORST currently teaches wildlife and nature photography at Colorado Mountain College, where his wife, **TRISH,** is pursuing a degree in business. Their prints are sold internationally through several galleries in Colorado.

Both are natives of Colorado and were raised with a high regard for nature. They became interested in photography while employed with the government in Alaska.

Upon return to their home state, Mr. Ramhorst obtained a degree in commercial photography, and they settled in the Rockies of Colorado. Their aim is to let their photos "help people become more attuned to the natural world around them which will result in a widespread commitment to preserve our environment."

ROBERT SMITH was born and raised in Clinton, South Carolina. He graduated in 1979 from the University of South Carolina, Columbia with a B.S. in accounting.

During the summer of 1980, Mr. Smith began working in Yellowstone National Park. He has been there ever since. "The beauty and diversity of the flora and fauna in Yellowstone Park has fascinated me since I moved here, and I don't think I could ever leave the park area," he says.

Robert Smith has achieved considerable success in his short two years of photography.

ADDITIONAL READINGS

TILDEN, FREEMAN. *The National Parks.* Alfred A. Knopf, New York. 1986.

UDALL, STEWART L. *The National Parks Of America.* G.P. Putnam's Sons, New York. 1966.

FISHER, RON. *Our Threatened Inheritance.* National Geographic Society, Washington, D.C. 1984.

National Geographic Society. *The Marvels Of Animal Behavior.* National Geographic Society, Washington, D.C. 1976.

FULLER, STEVEN and JEREMY SCHMIDT. *Yellowstone In Three Seasons.* Snow Country Publications, Yellowstone National Park. 1980.

SHAW, RICHARD G. *Wildflowers Of Yellowstone And Grand Teton National Parks.* Wheelwright Press, Ltd., Salt Lake City. 1976.

HARRY, BRYON and WILLARD E. DILLEY. *Wildlife Of Yellowstone And Grand Teton National Parks.* Wheelwright Press Ltd., Salt Lake City. 1972.

FOLLETT, DICK. *Birds Of Yellowstone And Grand Teton National Parks.* Roberts Rinehart, Inc., Boulder. 1985.

PETERSON, ROGER TORY. *A Field Guide To Western Birds.* Houghton Mifflin Company, Boston. 1961.

UDVARDY, MIKLOS D.F. *The Audubon Society Field Guide To North American Birds.* Alfred A. Knopf, New York. 1977.

JOHNSON, JOANNE M. and JIM KAHNWEILER. *Wild Familes.* Westcliffe Publishers Inc., Bozeman. 1985.

SCOTT, DOUGLAS M. and SUNI A. SCOTT. *Heritage From The Wild; Familiar Land And Sea Mammals Of The Northwest.* Northwest Geographer Series. 1985.

GILDART, ROBERT C. and JAN WASSINK. *Montana Wildlife.* Montana Magazine Inc., Helena. 1982.

National Parkways, A Photographic And Comprehensive Guide To Grand Teton National Park. National Parks Division of World-Wide Research and Publishing Co., Casper. 1976.

National Parkways, A Photographic And Comprehensive Guide To Yellowstone National Park. National Parks Division of World-Wide Research and Publishing Co., Casper. 1976.

A Guide To Grand Teton National Park, Wyoming. Division of Publications National Park Service, U.S. Dept. of the Interior Washington, D.C. 1984.

MC NULTY, TIM and PAT O'HARA. *Yellowstone National Park: Land Of Fire And Falling Water.* Woodlands Press, San Rafael. 1986.

LEOPOLD, ALDO. *A Sand County Almanac.* Oxford University Press, New York. 1949

MC FARLAND, DAVID. *The Oxford Companion To Animal Behavior.* Oxford University Press, New York. 1987.

HAINES, AUBREY L. *The Yellowstone Story.* Yellowstone Library & Museum Association in co-operation with Colorado Associated University Press, Yellowstone National Park. 1977.

C. F. Glover   Canon AE1P   Canon 70-210mm Lens, 1/250 sec. at f8   Bogen Tripod   64 Kodachrome

"THE GRAND" FROM ANTELOPE FLATS

We hope you've enjoyed *Secrets in Yellowstone & Grand Teton National Parks.*

If you would like to share this book with a friend please use the attached order form.

Thank you.

NATIONAL PHOTOGRAPHIC COLLECTIONS

O R D E R   F O R M

	Price per copy	Number of copies

Secrets in Yellowstone & Grand Teton National Parks

Softcover Edition **$19.95** × _____ = _____

Hardcover Edition **$29.95** × _____ = _____

Shipping & Handling for 1 book

Within the U.S. $ 3.00

Outside the U.S. $ 8.00

Each additional book add $ 1.50 × _____ = _____

Add 6% sales tax for Florida shipments: _____

Total Due   _____
(Please enclose check or money order)

Above prices effective until January 1, 1992, thereafter prices subject to change.

☐ Please advise me of future publications

Purchaser _____

Address _____

City _____ State _____ Zip _____

☐ Ship to (if different than above)

Name _____

Address _____

City _____ State _____ Zip _____

Send orders to:

National Photographic Collections
P.O. Box 31355, Palm Beach Gardens, FL 33410-7355

S U R V E Y

Would you take a minute to let us know which photographs you have chosen as your favorites? We will be printing posters on a limited number of photographs, based on your response. Thank you.

My favorite photographs are on pages:

_____ _____ _____ _____

NATIONAL PHOTOGRAPHIC COLLECTIONS

O R D E R   F O R M

	Price per copy	Number of copies

Secrets in Yellowstone & Grand Teton National Parks

Softcover Edition **$19.95** × _____ = _____

Hardcover Edition **$29.95** × _____ = _____

Shipping & Handling for 1 book

Within the U.S. $ 3.00

Outside the U.S. $ 8.00

Each additional book add $ 1.50 × _____ = _____

Add 6% sales tax for Florida shipments: _____

Total Due   _____
(Please enclose check or money order)

Above prices effective until January 1, 1992, thereafter prices subject to change.

☐ Please advise me of future publications

Purchaser _____

Address _____

City _____ State _____ Zip _____

☐ Ship to (if different than above)

Name _____

Address _____

City _____ State _____ Zip _____

Send orders to:

National Photographic Collections
P.O. Box 31355, Palm Beach Gardens, FL 33410-7355

S U R V E Y

Would you take a minute to let us know which photographs you have chosen as your favorites? We will be printing posters on a limited number of photographs, based on your response. Thank you.

My favorite photographs are on pages:

_____ _____ _____ _____